*SPLIT HORIZON*

# SPLIT HORIZON

## Thomas Lux

Houghton Mifflin Company

BOSTON NEW YORK 1994

Library of Congress Cataloging-in-Publication Data
Lux, Thomas, date.
Split horizon / Thomas Lux.
p.   cm.
ISBN 0-395-70098-1   ISBN 0-395-70097-3 (pbk)
I. Title.
PS3562.U87S67   1994
811'.54 — dc20   93-46333
                    CIP
Printed in the United States of America
BP 10 9 8 7 6 5 4 3 2 1

Book design by Melodie Wertelet

The author is grateful to the editors of the following magazines for permis-
sion to reprint the following poems: *Ackee:* Just Curious. *An American
Voice:* Proscribed. *The Atlantic Monthly:* Virgule, Gorgeous Surfaces. *The
American Poetry Review:* The People of the Other Village, Thrombosis
Trombone, Loudmouth Soup, River Blindness (Onchocerciasis), History
Books, Children in School During Heavy Snowfall. *Antaeus:* Onomato-
poeia. *The Chronicle of Higher Education:* Eyes Examined While You Wait.
*Field:* A Large Branch Splintered off a Tree in a Storm, Grim Town in a
Steep Valley. *The Greensboro Review:* A Boat in the Forest, Snow as the
Rain's Father. *Gulf Coast:* Kleptoparasite. *The Harvard Review:* A Streak of
Blood That Was Once a Tiny Red Spider. *The Iowa Review:* Fundamental,
Please Don't Touch the Ruins. *Midland Review:* Pecked to Death by
Swans, Glow Worm. *The New Yorker:* Cows. *Passages North:* The Driver
Ant, On Matters Ontological and Eschatological, Rhadamanthine, Irony.
*The Personal Crucifixion:* Biographies. *Ploughshares:* Frankly, I Don't Care.
*Phoebe:* Susanna Fontanarossa. *The Seneca Review:* Farmer Brown. *Three
Rivers:* Amiel's Leg. *TriQuarterly:* An Horatian Notion, Emily's Mom, "I
Love You Sweatheart," Autobiographical. *The Virginia Quarterly Review:*
Edgar Allan Poe Meets Sarah Hale (Author of "Mary Had a Little Lamb"),
Shaving the Graveyard, Endive. *Vox:* The Nazi at the Puppet Show, Job's
Problems.

   "Grim Town in a Steep Valley" also appeared in *Best American Poetry
1993* (Louise Glück, editor).
   Special thanks to Maria Elena Caballero-Robb and Pamela Cohn.

*— for Rachel*

I see at last that all the knowledge
I wrung from darkness — that the darkness flung me —
Is worthless as ignorance: nothing comes from nothing,
The darkness from darkness. Pain comes from the darkness
And we call it wisdom. It is pain.

— RANDALL JARRELL


. . . against which do not
Pray only but be vigilant and set your hand to the work.

— ALLEN GROSSMAN


. . . and one good lick of quicksand took.

— HEATHER MCHUGH

CONTENTS

*O N E*

hate the people of this village
and would nail our hats
to our heads for refusing in their presence to remove them
or staple our hands to our foreheads
for refusing to salute them
if we did not hurt them first: mail them packages of rats,
mix their flour at night with broken glass.
We do this, they do that.
They peel the larynx from one of our brothers' throats.
We devein one of their sisters.
The quicksand pits they built were good.
Our amputation teams were better.
We trained some birds to steal their wheat.
They sent to us exploding ambassadors of peace.
They do this, we do that.
We canceled our sheep imports.
They no longer bought our blankets.
We mocked their greatest poet
and when that had no effect
we parodied the way they dance
which did cause pain, so they, in turn, said our God
was leprous, hairless.
We do this, they do that.
Ten thousand (10,000) years, ten thousand
(10,000) brutal, beautiful years.

and was hurled to the ground like a spear.
In the morning there it stood, upright,
a new tree, twenty feet tall, sprung overnight.
Torn off with such force
it impales by several inches the grass and earth

and as I haul it out
I think: What if this very spot,
what were the chances — mathematically, spatially,
time-of-day-wise, cosmically — what odds
this spot could have been my wife's heart,

my baby's fontanel? Normal thinking
or normal (slash) paranoid?
I pull the branch — the white pith
of the wood stained by the wet earth — out,
bending to grip it at the base,

it was that deep. Torn from its source,
its leaves just beginning to wilt,
their gray backs closing like fists
around the greener fronts.
And then with my hatchet I hacked it up.

The thing gets made, gets built, and you're the slave
who rolls the log beneath the block, then another,
then pushes the block, then pulls a log
from the rear back to the front
again and then again it goes beneath the block,
and so on. It's how a thing gets made — not
because you're sensitive, or you get genetic-lucky,
or God says: Here's a nice family,
seven children, let's see: this one in charge
of the village dunghill, these two die of buboes, this one
Kierkegaard, this one a drooling

nincompoop, this one clerk, this one cooper.
You need to love the thing you do — birdhouse building,
painting tulips exclusively, whatever — and then
you do it
so consciously driven
by your unconscious
that the thing becomes a wedge
that splits a stone and between the halves
the wedge then grows, i.e., the thing
is solid but with a soul,
a life of its own. Inspiration, the donnée,

the gift, the bolt of fire
down the arm that makes the art?
Grow up! Give me, please, a break!
You make the thing because you love the thing
and you love the thing because someone else loved it

enough to make you love it.
And with that your heart like a tent peg pounded
toward the earth's core.
And with that your heart on a beam burns
through the ionosphere.
And with that you go to work.

They are, the surfaces, gorgeous: a master
pastry chef at work here, the dips and whorls,
the wrist-twist
squeezes of cream from the tube
to the tart, sweet bleak sugarwork, needlework
towards the perfect lace doily
where sit the bone china teacups, a little maze
of meaning maybe in their arrangement,
sneaky obliques, shadow
allusives all piling
atop one another. Textures succulent but famished,
banal, bereft. These surfaces,
these flickering patinas,
these gorgeous surfaces
through which,
if you could drill, or hack,
or break a trapdoor latch, if you could penetrate
these surfaces' milky cataracts, you
would drop,
free fall
like a hope chest full of lead,
to nowhere, no place, a dry-wind, sour,
*nada* place,
and you would keep dropping,
tumbling, slow
motion, over and over for one day, six days, fourteen
decades, eleven centuries (a long time
falling to fill a zero), and in that time
not a leaf, no rain,

not a single duck, nor hearts, not one human, nor sleep,
nor grace, nor graves — falling
to where the bottom, finally, is again the surface,
which is gorgeous,
which is glue, saw- and stone-dust, which is blue-gray
ice, which is
the barely glinting grit of abyss.

Rabbit tracks in an inch or so of new snow
have no origin (for who
follows tracks backwards?)
and have no end (the rabbit forever
moving ahead or disappears
into, say, a swamp). You pick
them up behind the corncrib, follow north
along the fenceline where he stopped, shook
a few seed pods off some dry weeds,
left some droppings (either because he had to

or to mark a territory: these are *my*
seeds, grim as they are, these are *mine*)
and then he cut due west, his straightest line yet,
across a pasture, exposed, his tracks wider,
running. A lean time, February,
for rabbits. He half-slid down a slit ravine,
his rump making a trough
through his tracks. Over
the small brook's center not frozen over
he must have leapt: deft

rabbit, hungry rabbit.
Then under the fallen bottom strand of barbwire
(a small tuft of gray-brown fur
points south on a north wind)
and into brush so thick
you cannot enter, though you try, a few yards.
You never saw him: ditto.
He never saw you: ditto.
And all the tracks behind, ahead overblown by a new inch
of snow: dot, dot, ditto.

What I love about this little leaning mark
is how it divides
without divisiveness. The left
or bottom side prying that choice up or out,
the right or top side pressing down upon
its choice: either/or,
his/her. Sometimes called a *slash* (too harsh), a *slant*
(a little dizzy but the Dickinson association
nice: "Tell the truth but tell it slant"), a *solidus* (sounding
too much like a Roman legionnaire
of many campaigns),
or a *separatrix* (reminding one of a sexual
variation). No, I like virgule. I like the word
and I like the function: "Whichever is appropriate
may be chosen to complete the sense."
There is something democratic
about that, grown-up; a long
and slender walking stick set against the house.
*Virgule:* it feels good in your mouth.
*Virgule:* its foot on backwards, trochaic, that's OK, American.
*Virgule:* you could name your son that,
or your daughter, *Virgula.* I'm sorry now
I didn't think to give my daughter such a name
though I doubt that she and/or
her mother would share that thought.

To go there: do not fall asleep, your forehead
on the footstool; do not have
your lunchpail dreams
or dreams so peaceful you hear leaves thud
into the fine silt at a river's edge;
do not hope you'll find it on this updraft
or that downdraft
in the airy airlessness.
It is elsewhere, elsewhere, the neighborhood you seek.
The neighborhood you long for,
where the gentle trolley — *ding, ding* — passes
through, where the adults are kind
and, better, sane,
that neighborhood is gone, no, never
existed, though it should have
and had a chance once
in the hearts of women, men (farmers dreamed
this place, and teachers, book writers, oh thousands
of workers, mothers prayed for it, hunchbacks,
nurses, blind men, maybe most of all soldiers,
even a few generals, millions
through the millennia . . .), some of whom,
despite anvils on their chests,
despite taking blow after blow across shoulders and necks,
despite derision and scorn,
some of whom still, *still*
stand up every day against ditches swollen with blood,
against ignorance, still dreaming,
full-fledged adults, still fighting,
trying to build a door to that place,
trying to pry open the ugly,
bullet-pocked, and swollen gate
to the other side,
the neighborhood of make-believe.

## EDGAR ALLAN POE MEETS SARAH HALE
## (AUTHOR OF "MARY HAD A LITTLE LAMB")


One would assume a difference in temperaments.
Their introduction likely took place at a lit'ry salon,
common in their day — Poe looking past her
at the punch bowl — or possibly they met
at the offices of *Godey's Lady's Book*, of which Sarah Hale
was an editor and for which
she purchased several stories (including
"The Purloined Letter") and sketches.
Because she knew — everybody knew — he needed cash
she paid him less than other authors,
knowing he'd take it. Business.
Nevertheless, Poe thought highly
enough of Hale to write: ". . . a lady of fine genius
and masculine energy and ability."
Was he aware of his patronizing? Unlikely.
Was he being obsequious? More likely.
He needed the money, being a drunk
and with a large laudanum habit.
Sarah Hale wrote a poem we all know.
The same is true for Mr. Edgar Allan Poe.

We were in a room that was once an attic,
the tops of the trees filled the windows, a breeze
crossed the table where we sat
and Amiel, about age four, came to visit
with her father, my friend,
and it was spring I think, and I remember
being happy — her mother was there too,
and my wife, and a few other friends.
It was spring, late spring, because the trees
were full but still that slightly lighter
green; the windows were open,
some of them, and I'll say it
out loud: I was happy, sober, at the time childless
myself, and it was one
of those moments: just like that, Amiel
climbed on my lap and put her head back against my chest.
I put one hand on her knees
and my other hand on top of that hand.
That was all, that was it.
Amiel's leg was cool, faintly rubbery.
We were there — I wish I knew the exact
date, time — and that
was all, that was it.

Did her name — of air and hills, like fat cream
on the tongue — did her name so full
of sibilants, assonance, the tender *oh*
near its end, did you ever
think of her name
as men usually don't
think of their mothers' names,

did you ever mouth her name
or say it alone on the deck of your ship
those mid-Atlantic nights five hundred years ago,
did her name fill your lungs
for a moment
and then the sails, did you call
her name as men sometimes do when fearful

though most often nearer death
and less determined than you,
Christopher Columbus?
In the pages of your journal her name does not appear.
In your century, as in ours,
this is not unusual
and goes unremarked upon, but her name,

her name so like a star chart, the gentle wash
in the sweet-water barrel, the white
river birds as first sign
of land, her name, Columbus,
did it help you navigate,
was it a heaven-marker upon which you set
your vain, cruel, and brilliant course?

## EXIT 5, 3 MILES: LORD'S VALLEY, GRUNDY'S CROSSING

At my present speed, 60 MPH, I have three minutes
to decide: do I take this exit — I want
to — and if I do (I need neither fuel
nor food), which way off it
do I turn? It'll be left, a mile
to Lord's Valley, a right 1.3 miles
to Grundy's Crossing. The Lord I like,
the notions thereof, I've heard of Him,
but is His valley wide enough,
and the river there (every valley
has its river): is it swift, clear, cool,
alive with fish? Will one more resident, transient,
tourist, pilgrim, be welcomed
there? Are the hillsides green, do the orchards groan
with fruit? My neighbors,
if I stay, will they love me?
And if I turn right, to Grundy's Crossing?
Crossing what: stream, lake, Suction Swamp?
Crossing *on* what: flat-bottom ferry, barge, rope bridge?
And crossing *to* what, on whatever other side —
Grundy's Landing, Grundytown, or -ville?
Two choices, less than a minute now.
Or three choices, a third: keep driving,
drive another thousand miles,
two, three,
until the road map pours out its roads
into a big blank — aside from the odd
island — jagged blue.

Trochee, trochee, trochee — that's how
I heard them, the cows,
their beings, they walked
like that, into the barn each night
and out again each morning after giving up their milk.
They were always eating, their heads down,
in field or barn,
eating grass or grain.
The field short-cropped, lunar,
dotted with rocks,
cow pies. Out of thirty, maybe three
or four you gave names
to: Bossy, Bessy. They were stupid
not cute, and would not love or nuzzle you.
They went out in the morning and came back at dusk.
They didn't just hand it over,
their milk, but you could take it from them,
great foamy pails
emptied into vats
and sold for cash, all but one large blue pitcherful,
which stayed home
and which, when cold,
you poured atop a bowl of oatmeal
and ate through a thousand winters, every day
safe, tame, broken, and lost.

Vodka, whisky, gin. Scotch. Red wine, cognac,
brandy — are you getting thirsty yet? — ale,
rye. It all tastes good: on the rocks, with a splash,
side of soda, shaken
not stirred, triple
olives, one of those nutritious little pearl
onions, a double, neat,
with a twist. Drink
it up, let's have *a* drink: dry beer, wet beer,
light, dark, and needled beer. Oh parched,
we drank the river
nearly to its bed at times, and were so numb
a boulder on a toe
was pleasant pain, all pain
was pleasant since that's all there was, pain,
and everything that was deeply felt, deeply,
was not. Bourbon, white and pink wine, *apéritif*,
cordial (hardly!), cocktail, martini,
highball, *digestif*, port, grain
punch — are you getting thirsty yet? — line them up!
We'll have *a* drink
and talk, we'll have
*a* drink and sleep, we'll
have *a* drink
and die, grim-about-it-with-piquancy.
It was a long time on the waiting list
for zero
and I'm happy
for the call out of that line
to other, less predictable,
more joyful
slides to ride on home.

If I mix a vegetable and moral metaphor
then this pale,
arrogant little leaf — its juices spare,
its taste pinched
and numbing — is equivalent
to a rich child pulling legs
off a bug, to a swaggering walk through a TB ward
by a pulmonary giant. Not to mention
a pathetic excuse for salad: four, five spiked shards
arranged like spokes
around its hub: a radish delicately carved.
The white plate upon which it sits so bare it blinds me.
Who, forced to wear white butler's gloves,
bends over a row all day
to pick this for a lousy wage
and can't afford or, I'd prefer, refuses
to eat it? It's so pallid
turning to yellow, I feel stabbing it
with my fork
would hurt it
or at least be impolite
so I slide the shiny tines beneath a piece
and lift it to my lips
and it's as if I'm eating air
but with a slight afterburn: dust and bone,
privilege and toe dancing.
So delicate, curling in on itself
in an ultimate self-embrace: fussy, bitter, chaste, clerical
little leaf.

By day he worked at pumping gas, oil changes,
clean-your-windshield — to keep it going
so he could cut his hay, or plow, at night.
It is the way small farmers make it.
He wasn't an insomniac,
that you can bet. He would say
he preferred the dark to work his fields:
*A tractor's got lights, it's cooler
then . . . my eyezur good.*
Long after the longest day
I'd watch his tractor's double beams
slice the dark, forth and back, tilting
on hillsides until I was called to sleep.
I suppose he finished in time to milk
his cows and then to sleep himself
before he went to work. The few times
I actually saw him he wore
mechanic's overalls with an oval
above his heart: *Malcolm.* Malcolm Brown,
a farmer's perfect name, and if
he did not know this, he did know
what he had to do: work by night, work by day,
eating a sandwich with one hand.
He owned his cows and he kept his land.
Farmer Brown, farmer Malcolm Brown,
I praise you, who are probably dead by now,
and if, by luck or mercy of the banks,
you are not, I praise your work — moonlit,
washed by black — and I praise the land
you work on, which I hope you own today, outright.

Acts of God,
the insurance people, whose business depends
on fear of them,
call them: hurricane, monsoon, cyclone,
whirlwind — when your house bears
the branches' lash, big winds
lift and slam the clapboards.
Little spiders, spirit receptors,
living in the walls or swinging
above the sills, sense it
first, are humble. The fiery,
the fundamental God
is mad, again. He gets that way,
decides to smash or flood
and it's no use to build a sandbag wall
around your acre, to try to divert
the torrents via channel
dug by hand. Or, He says: No water,
not a drop. I'll burn
their legumes to dust,
swell and crack their black black tongues.
Oh no — fire ants, weevil, mouse plague,
locusts: with a hundred neighbors
we'll beat the fields with rakes
and brooms — hopeless, hopeless — but our effort
saves a few more loaves
for winter — until God gives them mold: Cold *and*
hungry, He says. He says: These bugs
are tiny and bad,
mostly, I don't like their habits — so greedy,

mean, what'll shape them up
is fire and noise, their fields
I'll burn and barren,
what they need are heaps of pumice,
ash up to their ears,
and their sky, under my feet,
their sky, bloody and wracked, I'll split with howls.

You must not, no matter how deep — up to your knees,
waist — in bees and yellow and caress, a gravel avalanche
of hormonal noises in your loins, you must not,
it is forbidden to hold one another like that (lips to lips
or secret parts, no, no), the law

is clear, interpreted, no,
don't look, don't touch,
it is unclean. The penalties
are just, merciless: your nose
to fall off, your penis, that vile slug,

to become a dog
which gnaws your belly, your breasts (your breasts,
all breasts are forbidden!) barren, your children,
impure issue, to turn their hands against you,
your father to gouge out your heart

while you dream your mother loves you. . . .
It is easy to be happy here: obey.
Obey, a godly word, say yourself to sleep
with it and let it be the word
that burns your lips at dawn: obey.

# FRANKLY, I DON'T CARE

> This miserable scene demands a groan.
> —JOHN GAY


Frankly, I don't care if the billionaire is getting divorced
and thus boosting the career
of his girlfriend, a "model/spokesperson" with no job
and nothing to promote; nor does my concern
over celebrity X undergoing surgical procedures,
leaked as "primarily cosmetic" if it can be measured
quantitatively, reach the size of the space
inside a hollow needle. Regardless,
prayer vigils are being held
around the clock in the hospital lobby.
It's not that I wish
for a slip of the surgeon's wrist
but I just flat-simple don't care
although I understand and try
to empathize: as beauty diminishes
so does the bankroll. I am also indifferent
to — to the point of yawns large enough
to swallow the world — a senator's or, say, singer's
girlfriend's or boyfriend's disclosures
re the singer's or senator's sexual behavior — well, unless
the disclosure is *explicitly* detailed
and for christsake *interesting!*
— But does this protest too much?
We the people, day-laboring citizens, need to love
those of you larger than us, those whose teeth
are like floodlights against loneliness,
whose great gifts of song, or for joke telling,
or thespianly sublime transformations
take us, for whole moments at a time, away
from ourselves. We need

you and from this point on we promise
to respect your privacy,
diminish our demands on you,
never to take pleasure
in your troubles or pain.
And on those cruel days when death has its way
and takes two or even three of you
at once, three of more or less equal fame, we will,
in the obituaries, the newscasts, the front pages,
we will list your departures alphabetically;
your popularity will not, on this day, be tallied
or polled. Because in death, although still not anonymous,
you will be like us: small,
equal, voiceless, and gone.

# THE DRIVER ANT

Every member of the army is completely blind.

— JOHN COMPTON, *on the driver ant*

Eats meat exclusively. Can't bear
direct sunlight, marches at night,
in tall grass, or in covered causeways
it builds, by day. Relentless,
nervous, short, conservative,
twenty million or more,
like a thick black living rope
they exit, often, the colony
to eat: lizards, guanas, monkeys,
rats, mice, the tasty
largest python, *Python natelensis,*
who just devoured a small antelope
and can't move: double dinner,
in a few hours a pile of bones
inside a pile of bones.
This army's slow
(one meter per three min.) so
they can't catch you
unless you're lame,
or dumb, or staked
to the ground — a hard way to die,
eating first your eyes,
and then too many mandibles
clean you to your spine.
The Driver Ant, penniless,
goes out to eat
in hoards, in rivers, in armies of need,
good citizens
serving a famished state.

*T W O*

were really one problem: the God he chose
was capricious, cruel, cold,
and a windbag, yammer, yammer,
a fine poet (or his ghostwriter) but a windbag,
braggart. Hurt, He said,
hurt Job terribly,
kill (and they need not
be mentioned again) his ten children,
pile boil upon boil upon his back,
program the locust to gnaw away his nose,
but don't
let him die, I'll want to rub some salt in
later. . . . Not death,
just torture: now there's a God
to whom you want to give your heart.
As Maimonides said: Job was a good man,
but stupid. As were his friends Bildad,
Eliphaz, and Zophar: boneheads,
mewly aphorists, boot lickers, greeting card
optimists, and them too — yammer, yammer.
And Job had some breath to expend himself,
a gift for metaphor,
simile. Also ego
and self-effacement (where is the latter
really the former?), and then God,
insecure, piqued,
deigns to speak
from within a whirlwind
and is, of course, the better poet
though his work flawed by arrogance
and also too oblique.

Maybe he's more afraid of being understood,
as Nietzsche said
of certain philosophers,
than he is of being *mis*understood.
Job, nevertheless, is impressed, submits.
God, his ego salved,
first rebukes Bildad, Eliphaz, and Zophar
(no protest from them), then
gives back, twofold, Job's sheep, camels, cows,
provides seven new sons and three new daughters,
daughters very beautiful
and with very exotic names,
not Joan, or Betty, or Jane.
And, God gave Job
the famous 140 more years
(on top of how many already?), which means
he outlived his wife
and second family
and died rich, and happy, and alone.

The patient children stand in line
to be counted, to be assigned
their seats by height: the short up front,
taller to the rear. November, frozen puddles
shine like the eyes of a somnambulist
if you lift his lids. Needle wind.
The Nazi, a dead-serious
doorkeeper, a functionary

at the puppet show,
takes the tickets, slow,
up and down the line
and tears each one
at the angle of a guillotine
but will not let the children in.
They do not wail or whine.
They're here to see the show in which the rabbit

outwits the crocodile and is not
eaten. To see that, they will bear a lot.
The Nazi blocks the door, checks her watch.
Inside, over a candle,
the puppeteer warms his hands.
And the puppets lie as still and blind
as wood, as buttons, as cloth
in their blue-black box.

# KALASHNIKOV

(an AK-47 assault rifle, probably the most
numerous small-arms weapon in history)


Designed by Mikhail Kalashnikov who, if alive
today, is seventy-three years old,
but is he
as well known in his native Russia
as Marina Tsvetayeva, Anna Akhmatova,
or Osip Mandelstam? Russians love
their poets. I don't know

how they feel about Kalashnikov
but he is or was wealthier
than the poets above ever were
and has out there several million
of his namesakes: read a book
in which people shoot people — revolutionaries,
whether earnest, sincere,

or just thugs: Kalashnikovs, everybody's got one.
There's a guerrilla
somewhere: a Kalashnikov. Assassins,
warlords' soldiers, smugglers, pirates,
poachers: Kalashnikovs, caliber
7.62 x 39,600 rounds
per minute, a potential 10 corpses

per second.
Kalashnikov — it's not a dance,
nor a troupe of funny jugglers,
nor is it a vodka,
and if you said a small city (pop. 49,000)
in the southern Crimea,
you'd be stone-dead wrong.

## THE LIMBIC SYSTEM

(from *limbus:* an edge, fringe, or border)


The brain matter beneath the brain stem
and millimeters below the neocortex: imprecisely
defined, mysterious, no one
expert enough to know
for sure but having to do
with the visceral,
the emotional status of the organism: fear
and anger,
flight and defense, sense
of smell. . . . One part called *gyrus fornicatus*
and others called hippocampus,
uncus, amygdala. It is an injustice
that only neuro-doctors
get to say these words
and visit these places, map them, decode them.
And yet we all live there
where it is most primal, neurons firing
like starbursts, like the first flint
struck at night by hand on another stone — we all
live there near an edge,
just across the border
from another country,
the next: time.

The latest research: left-handedness
is a form of brain damage. That's nice
to know, thank you very much.
From the Latin: *sinistrum* = sinister = evil = left.
If you use the wrong arm: more migraines, more likely

to stutter, more likely dyslexia. Females,
both human and monkey, tend to carry offspring
in their left arm, thereby leaving free the right hand
to stroke or pamper them.
If you use the wrong arm: you perform poorly

on verbal tests: *I knowed that.*
And Matthew (of Matthew, Mark, Luke . . .) says: The sheep
on the right hand go to heaven
and those on the left go to hell.
If you use the wrong arm: you live less

long, nine years, on average.
Six times more likely to die in accidents (in general),
four times more likely to die in accidents (specific: cars): if
you use the wrong arm.
If you use the wrong arm: more likely eczema, diabetes,

sleep disorders, epilepsy, schizophrenia. . . .
If you use the wrong arm: cut it off.
If you use the wrong arm: be cautious.
If you use the wrong arm: take care
not to believe all that you read.

# MONEY

A paper product. We say it's green
but it's not, it's slate green, drained green.
New, it smells bad
but we like to sniff it
and when we have a relative pile
we not only want to inhale it but also look at it,
hear it buzz
as we work with our thumbs
its corners like a deck of cards.
A wall of it would be nice, in bricks
like you see in the movies
when vaults get robbed.
And those beautiful — so tiny — red, blue threads,
capillaries, cilia, embedded
in the texture of the paper (that secret
which most thwarts the phony money men),
those threads
like river valleys on a distant planet,
rivers with no end, no source,
like steep ravines in an otherwise flat pan
of a landscape. Look long
and deep enough
at a piece of paper money
and you will see the heaven you were promised,
there, which we look so hard into,
to the very bottom, depths of which
we are called
by the riverbed, the ravine's bleached stones
calling us down: money, money,
paper money.

gets made up of 5.3 billion little pictures (sacks, thousands,
of rice rotting, rat-gnawed, in warehouses, jail cell
graffiti, a tiny crimson powder-burned disc
on a man's forehead, a torturer's migraine, immense
abstract delusions — "no problem here" — a filthy

fingernail sunk in a chunk of gray bread . . .), eleven pictures
of medium size (the Marxist discussion group
breaks down into smaller groups
to study punctuational/syntactical nuances, why nobody
minds lies if they are colossal enough, etc.), a few blank

frames (example: Jesus walking on water and rising
from the dead?, the Mormon guy, Joe Smith — sounds like
an alias — digging up some gold plates
in his backyard?: this enumeration, this list
of mysteries could go on and on

without *ever any* verification . . .), a few ruined
snapshots (a chicken in every BBQ, social justice), one
shattered vision, a few mild
auditory hallucinations, faint harp
music, celestial crowing

or choiring, or the low love cooing
of an amorous duo,
Ignorance and Certainty, that each lost one of us,
I pray, would agree, should agree, should be
sterilized!

This valley: as if a huge, dull, primordial ax
once slammed into the earth
and then withdrew, innumerable millennia ago.
A few flat acres
ribbon either side of the river sliding sluggishly
past the clock tower, the convenience store.
If a river could look over its shoulder,
glad to be going, this one would.
In town center: a factory of clangor and stink,
of grinding and oil,
hard howls from drill bits
biting sheets of steel. All my brothers
live here, every cousin, many dozens
of sisters, my worn aunts
and numb uncles, the many many of me,
a hundred sad wives,
all of us countrymen and -women
born next to each other behind the plow
in this valley, each of us
pressing to our chests a loaf of bread
and a jug of milk. . . . The river is low
this time of year and the bedstones' blackness
marks its lack
of depth. A shopping cart
lies on its side in center stream
gathering branches, detritus, silt,
forcing the already weak current to part for it,
dividing it, but even so diminished
it's glad to be going,
glad to be gone.

In bad shape, buried
3,500 years, the ruins, nevertheless,
are beautiful: I take the tour.
Their houses were crude, and the people,
judged by door frames, short.
They had many jars. Their island green
and their harbor safe.

Half-excavated, not much to see,
the tin roof over the dig
keeps it dark amid the dust,
their art packed off to museums.
Boxes and boxes of shards
remain — must be millions — and is someone
going to fit them all together again?

I'd like to lift just one, but the guards
won't allow you a pebble
in your shoe. The tiny
citizens living here were painterly,
prosperous, and all escaped
(not a human femur found)
the lava and the ash — as, often,

people did before eruption, tidal wave,
invader, though not from famine or plague.
Where did they go in their baby boats,
did they pack their jars with oil
and barley, where did they sail
without their art and larger animals?
Little long-agos, the sign says

not to touch your ruins.
I won't. And were the mainland museum
open when I went there,
I would have seen your art
other than on postcards or cheap gifts:
they moved me very much,
your ebullient blue monkeys and fish.

The problem is: even for a long life — Tolstoy, say —
they are too short: 100 pages, or less,
equals 10 years! And 3,650-plus days
gone to an ounce or so of pages flipped
in a few hours — how many inhalations unmentioned,
sore elbows, brief quakes of despair,
good kisses unrecorded? And the great deeds,
the battles, the landfall, the lover found
whom the poem or novel
rearranges into art — a relative few
pages. All is known, nothing
is known, since the narrative of a life
cannot be
but only be about
the life. Take biographies of writers, for example,
books about people who wrote books
good enough other writers not only want to write books
about their books
but also about their lives which, in one way or another,
are what their books are about.
Here's Pound, the poet/megalomaniac, writing 9,000
frantic letters and postcards about money: "Have you ever
thought about money, what makes it,
and how it got that way?"
Or Dickinson upstairs in her room — doing what?
Not pining for some lover, that's for sure.
No, writing poems that made a lot of people
want to read them
and some people want to write her biography.
Decades pass neatly with chapters, the subjects' parents die,
divorces, illnesses, the author seeks,
explicates insights, turning points,
that which *specifically*

makes a life a life
worth a book. . . .
Turgenev mooning over some singer: decades!
Father Hopkins: did he love his pal in college?
Henry Miller: *always* broke,
until he was so old and so known for being broke
that when he got some money he still felt he *should* be broke.
Does the reader get a better deal
from a short life/long bio
or a long life/long bio?
First come lives.
Then come books — those gifts.
Then come books about books.
And then come books about people who wrote books
which you do not *need* to read
but you do,
loving them for having written books
you love.

This creature, like all creatures, holds a certain niche
(for which a metaphor exists) in nature: to pick
the predator's pocket. The predator kills
something — stalks, chases, snaps its neck, punctures
its jugular — and this thing steals it.
Nice work if you can get it. It's a life,

a living, though not without its risks: the predator
(for whom a metaphor exists) would prefer
to keep and eat his prey
himself, becomes annoyed,
does not want
to give over even part

of what he worked so hard
and killed for: food.
And don't confuse
the kleptoparasite with a scavenger, or bone picker,
or an ingratiating, patient crumb eater: it wants
it all, the whole carcass

(for which a metaphor exists), fresh, warm,
all or most of the best parts intact.
The kleptoparasite
needs to eat,
knows no other way — adapted, evolved down
from a predator or up

from a scavenger,
the scientists can't tell which,
since the problem with the empirical, the literal,
is that it is
empirical,
literal.

First, a female buffalo gnat of the genus *Simulium* bites you
and in the process
deposits her infective larvae.
In ten to twenty months (no big hurry) they grow
to threadlike adult worms
which live up to fifteen years under the skin,
intermuscularly, in fascial planes, against the capsules
of joints or the shafts of long bones — the neighborhoods
they love inside you. The adult females,
now residing in your body, produce live embryos
which live a year or two,
migrating, restless,
during which time they will likely invade your eyes,
lymph glands, or other (you don't want to know
which) organs. Results
are unpleasant: blindness, which might be merciful,
for then you don't see: rash, wheals, gross
lichenification, atrophy (known as "lizard skin"),
enlarged lymph glands
leading to pockets of loose flesh,
"hanging groins," which predispose
to hernia, and so on.
Treatment: Serious drugs, some so toxic the treatment worse
than the illness.
Prognosis: If you are not reinfected, the parasites die out
within fifteen years. Symptoms of disease, however, may
get worse during this time.
Prevention: Avoid Third World communities,

particularly those located within twenty kilometers
of fast-flowing rivers
in which *Simulium* prefers to breed.
Some twenty to forty million (hard to be exact!) people infected,
baby flies dying, dying
in their eyes,
blinding them.

About the river disanimated, running in reverse,
refusing a ride to seed pods, twigs,
charging rent to its fish, exiling
its currents. I'm curious
about the dead middle of a black star, something's
going on in there where each gnawed dream goes.
That metallic object,

X-shaped — I'm curious about it — growing
in the president's brain, the pins
in his heart too, how
did they get there? And the simulacra
everywhere: nailed up on trees
are pictures of trees?
I've always

been curious, born that way — why this,
why that — in a hayloft,
on the playground: *Macaroni, macaroni,*
*the teacher's a phony*
*and I love my books only* — why
did you say that, why
did you ask that? I'm just curious:

Who can the self-made man worship but his creator?
Why harness a horse to a load he cannot haul?
I'm just curious, I can't help it,
and the answers, the data-truth,
luckily, the information,
is everywhere
and cheap.

*(Summer 1992)*

That is, their authors, leave out
one thing: the smell. How sour, no, rancid — bad cheese
and sweat — the narrow corridors of Hitler's bunker
during the last days powdered
by plaster shaken down
under bomb after bomb. Or (forward or backward
through time, history books take you) downstream
a mile or two from a river-crossing ambush
a corpse washes ashore
or catches in branches
and bloats in the sun. The carrion eaters
who do not fly
come by their noses: the thick,
ubiquitous, sick, sweet smell.
Most of history, however,
is banal, not bloody: the graphite and wood smell
of a pencil factory, the glue- fertilizer- paper-
(oh redolent!) shoe- hat- (ditto malodor
*and* poisonous) chemical- salt cod-
munitions- canning- shirtwaist- plastics- box-
tractor- etc. factories — and each one
peopled by people: groins, armpits, feet.
A bakery, during famine; guards, smoking, by the door.
Belowdecks, two years out, dead calm, tropics.
And wind a thousand miles all night combing
the tundra: chilled grasses, polar bear droppings,
glacial exhalations . . . Open
the huge book of the past: *whoosh!*: a staggering cloud
of stinks, musks

and perfumes, swollen pheromones, almond
and anise, offal dumps, mass graves exhumed, flower
heaps, sandalwood bonfires, milk vapors
from a baby's mouth, all of us
wading hip-deep through the endless
waftings, one bottomless soup
of smells: primal, atavistic — sniff, sniff, sniff.

# THREE
## Other Voices

The graveyard being what he called his face;
even as a young man
he called his face the graveyard — he talked
like that, funny, odd
things that scared me sometimes

in our early years. I thought maybe he was a little touched
(his Uncle Bob was certifiable)
but it was just his way of talking. *U-feeisms*,
he told me once, he liked to use *u-feeisms*,
which was no language

I ever heard of. He never touched a drop, though,
nor ever lifted a hand against me
or the kids, and when it came to loving,
well, he was sweet, but talking strange then
too: Bug Sauce, he'd call me, or Lavender Limbs,

or sometimes Birdbath — never Honey
or Sugar like other husbands when they talked, talked.
He was funny like that. Anyway,
after breakfast (he always shaved *after* breakfast,
said his face was "looser" then)

he'd stroke his chin and say:
*Time to shave the graveyard*,
and he would and then he'd go to work,
the handle of his lunchpail hooked through
with a belt and slung

over his shoulder. Some days I'd watch him
until he reached the corner
of Maple and Cottage
where he turned and walked the two blocks
to the mill.

The minute my brother gets out of jail I want
some answers: when our mother
murdered our father
did she find out first, did he tell her — the pistol's tip
parting his temple's fine hairs — did he
tell her where our sister (the youngest, Alice)
hid the money Grandma (mother's side)
stole from her Golden Age Group?
It was a lot of money but *enough to die for?*
was what Mom said she asked him,
giving him a choice. *I'll see you in hell,*
she said Dad said
and then she said (this is in the trial transcript): *Not
any time soon, needle dick!*
We know Alice hid the money — she was arrested

a week later in Tacoma for armed robbery,
which she would not have done
if she had it. Alice was (she died
of a heroin overdose six hours after making bail)
syphilitic, stupid, and rude
but not greedy. So she hid the money,
or Grandma did,
but since her stroke can't say a word,
doesn't seem to know anybody.
Doing a dime at Dannemora
for an unrelated sex crime, my brother
might know something but won't answer
my letters, refuses to see me,
though he was the one who called me
at divinity school

after Mom was arrested. He could hardly
get the story out from laughing
so much: Dad had missed
his third in a row the day before with his parole officer,
the cops were sent
to pick him up (*Bad timing,* said Mom) and found him
before he was cold.
*He was going back to jail anyway,* Mom said,
said the cops,
which they could and did use against her
to the tune of double digits, which means,
what with the lupus, she's guaranteed
to die inside. Ask her?
She won't talk to me.
She won't give me the time of day.

## ON MATTERS ONTOLOGICAL
## AND ESCHATOLOGICAL

You mean the being business, today's news,
and when you put your tongue
as if it were a blind man
on her braille, or how the sun this morning settles
in the crater of a spoon — you can *see*
this, it exists: the silver scratches
are river valleys, you can
see this, your eyes are working,
there is a cup, an orange.
Professor, why do you talk that way?
What lure the polysyllables
when they mean alive or dead, or egg yolk, wrist hairs?
Professor, what do you mean by the *nature*
of being, existence? How high, in millimeters, the egg yolk
sits, or does the egg yolk exist
for man (no fair x-ray
or infrared) while still inside
the egg? Or the tensile properties
or at what height one wrist hair crosses
its neighbor? Professor, does your wife
still love you? Or your students, do their numbers
at your lectures dwindle
since your tenure? And does tenure, professor,
have to do with matters
escha . . . eschatolo . . . the matters last or final,
the afterlife matters — I would like to know
about them. Say I die Friday night
after the dance, Susan doesn't love me anymore, I hurl
myself from a water tower, my pals later
banging their foreheads on the coffin . . .
When Susan dies fifty, sixty years hence
will I be my age now in the spirit-place
and she an old woman,
and will she be (still be) sorry when we meet?

Will we touch or walk right through each other?
The being business, professor, just look around, lift
your face from the page — but the other,
the after, the ether-fuzzy,
the cave-with-no-torches, talk about it, tell me
about that.

Our second winter here, plus a spring, summer,
fall, and how many will survive
What's His Name only knows.
All our ship's stores gone, every cracker, candle, keg
of salt fish we salvaged
before the ice broke her up
and took her down, all but the top
twenty feet of mast
like a pathetic Yuletide tree
growing from the frozen bay. Nine died
by spring — worst, the surgeon, by opium.
The captain died right off, the mate
wandered into a whiteout, gone.
We killed some food that summer: seals, fish,
some bitter, oily birds.
More died. A boy was taken by wolves.
Our larder's low: dried meat, fish.
Firewood for half the winter,
if we half-freeze, part of which is the mast
we hacked from the ice.
May the Lord send over some sandwiches soon
since we are starving here in the New World
with no clear passage to the Old,
no good slaves to be sold,
no silver, and there is not to be had
a single ingot of gold.

## PECKED TO DEATH BY SWANS

*— for Stephen Dobyns*

Your tear-wracked family bedside: elderly grandchildren,
great-grandchildren arriving
straight from med school; not a peep of pain, calm,
lucid, last words impeccably drafted?

No. Pecked to death by swans.

Having saved the lives of twelve crippled children
(pulled from a burning circus tent), the president
calling your hospital room, and you say: *Tell him
to call back;* all the opiate drugs you want?

No. Pecked to death by swans.

Great honors accrued, *Don't go* telegram from the pope
on the side table, serious lobby
already in place re a commemorative stamp; a long
long life capped by falling, peacefully, asleep?

No. I said: Pecked to death by swans.

By a bullet meant for a lover or a best friend,
by a car set to kill someone else whom you pushed,
because you could, out of the way; the ululations
of a million mourners rising to your window?

No. Pecked to death by swans.

## THE RIVER THAT SCOLDS
## AT ALL THE OTHER RIVERS

This bossy river, its rate of descent a degree or two greater
than its neighbors, its bed
of bigger stones — *Oh rounder, more smooth,* it seems
to say, *my alluvium*
*so much richer* — this river is angry now, in spring,
bragging, after a winter of heavy snow
in the mountains. *On I go with more urgency*
*than you,* it says to the little river that runs parallel
for so many miles, *you will be part of me,*
*I will eat you soon.* And the smaller river
does, is, that is, becomes a part of it, and the larger
larger, bossier still. *My path*
*the best path, my notch, my groove*
*the most true, says the river, I will*
*eat my banks, bow my own bends;*
*the shortest distance between two points,*
*that's how I go and haul*
*with me whatever is in my way,*
*taking it all: the trees, and men*
*in tissuey canoes, the ice, the rain,*
*the moon on my back, everything,*
*louder and louder as I go, the dwellings*
*that line me, the bridges that cross me,*
*everything, louder and louder,*
*faster as I roll, as I tear*
*right into the arms, back into the belly — nothing*
*can stop me — of my mother again.*

*F O U R*

(Emily Norcross Dickinson, 1804–1882,
mother of Emily Elizabeth Dickinson, 1830–1886)


Today we'd say she was depressed, clinically. Then,
they called it "nameless disabling apathy," "persistent nameless
infirmity," "often she fell sick
with nameless illnesses and wept
with quiet resignation." *The Nameless*, they should
have called it! She was *depressed*,
unhappy, and who can blame her
given her husband, Edward, who was, without exception,
absent — literally and otherwise — and in comparison
to a glacial range, cooler by a few degrees.
Febrile, passionate: not Edward.
"From the first she was desolately lonely."
A son gets born, a daughter (the poet), another daughter,
and that's all, then nearly fifty years
of "tearful withdrawal and obscure maladies."
She was depressed, for christsake! The Black Dog
got her, the Cemetery Sledge, the Airless Vault,
it ate her up
and her options few: no Prozac then, no Elavil,
couldn't eat *all* the rum cake,
divorce the sluggard?
Her children? Certainly they
brought her some joy?: "I always ran home to Awe
when a child, if anything befell me. He was an Awful Mother,
but I liked him better than none."
This is what her daughter, the poet, said.
No, it had her,
for a good part of a century
it had her by the neck: the Gray Python,
the Vortex Vacuum.
During the last long (seven) years,
crippled further by a stroke,

it did not let go but, *but*: "We were never intimate
Mother and children while she was our Mother
but mines in the ground meet by tunneling
and when she became our Child, the Affection came."
This is what Emily, her daughter, wrote
in that manner wholly hers,
the final word
on Emily, her mother — melancholic,
fearful, starved-of-love.

"MR JOHN KEATS FIVE FEET TALL"
SAILS AWAY


on the *Maria Crowther*,
a cargo brig
of 127 tons bound for Italy,
Naples, the sun
which was thought would cure his cough, his lungs.
The day: Sunday, 17 September 1820.
With him: Severn,
a painter, his nurse-companion;
Mrs. Pidgeon, a pain in the ass
and cold; Miss Cotterell,
like Keats consumptive
and "very lady-like but a sad martyr
to her illness," wrote Severn;
the captain and crew.
This was not a pleasure cruise.
Second day out: the sick
and nonsick get seasick
and "bequeath to the mighty sea their breakfasts."
Storms, water by the pailful
in the sleeping cabin; calms, nary a puff.
A squall (Bay of Biscay),
a calm again (Cape Saint Vincent),
then, one dawn, Gibraltar, the African coast!
Then, Bay of Naples,
Saturday, 21 October — ten days
quarantined
during which not one porthole opened
it rained so hard and long.
Welcome, Mr. Keats, to sunny southern Italy.
Then, by wagon, on roads ripe
with malaria, to Rome
from where in the two months plus
he still has lungs

he does not write again to Fanny Brawne,
whom he loves,
though he does write about
her to a friend
the famous sentence: "Oh God! God! God!" (in whom
he had no faith) "Every thing
I have in my trunk
reminds me of her
and goes through me like a spear."
And the better but less quoted
next sentence: "The silk
lining she put in my travelling cap scalds
my head." The verb choice "scalds"
perfect here (literally he had the fever,
figuratively . . .), the tactility
fresher, the melodrama cut
by an almost comic hyperbole. It is
more Keats than Keats,
who died 172 years, 8 months, 2 weeks, and 4 days
ago — this tiny man
John Keats,
who wrote some poems
without which,
inch by inch — in broken
barn light,
in classrooms (even there!),
under the lamp where what you read
teaches you what you love — without which
we would each,
inch by hammered inch,
we would each
be diminished.

## BOATS

> Being in a ship is being in a jail, with the chance
> of being drowned.
>
> — SAMUEL JOHNSON

Or, being in a boat is like being in a coffin,
alive, that floats — for the time being,
most of the time. You're in a rowboat, four yards
from shore, water waist-deep
and the floorboards damp: I did not want to die this way!
You like, though, how the shipwrecks look
through the modern deep-sea camera lens, especially
if they sit, as they sometimes do, on their bottoms
on the bottom: all fuzzy
and wavy with weeds, crustaceous
and silty. Underwater ghost towns
in which the furtive fish enter,
exit portholes . . . "The dice
of drowned men's bones," Hart Crane wrote, connoting
chance, a gamble
sailors take when they go to work: living things
are meant to live in,
not on, the water. The famous shipwrecks: *Titanic,*
*Lusitania, S.S. Priscilla,*
*Andrea Doria* — you've heard of them,
which were never supposed to sink
but did,
leaving their drowned bobbing like twigs
or else bug-eyed
and floating near the ceilings of their cabins,
food for fish,
lost to the dirt or fire we're supposed to go to
if we don't go down to
the lake, stream, pond, river, bayou, etc., in boats.

A man risked his life to write the words.
A man hung upside down (an idiot friend
holding his legs?) with spray paint
to write the words on a girder fifty feet above
a highway. And his beloved,
the next morning driving to work . . . ?
His words are not (meant to be) so unique.
Does she recognize his handwriting?
Did he hint to her at her doorstep the night before
of "something special, darling, tomorrow"?
And did he call her at work
expecting her to faint with delight
at his celebration of her, his passion, his risk?
She will *know* I love her now,
the *world* will know my love for her!
A man risked his life to write the words.
Love is like this at the bone, we hope, love
is like this, Sweatheart, all sore and dumb
and dangerous, ignited, blessed — always,
regardless, no exceptions,
always in blazing matters like these: blessed.

## A STREAK OF BLOOD THAT
## ONCE WAS A TINY RED SPIDER

is all there is left of it which walked
down the page of a book
and which I meant only to brush away
but crushed
to this minuscule skid mark — 4 mm high, ½ mm wide: baby
red scar, somewhat askew

hyphen forever
on page 211 of *Lost Tribes and Promised Lands.*
It had many legs — it was moving fast.
Some version of a heart must have been in there.
Some sensory talents.
Descending down a page,

little literate one, you came to the end of your page,
and thus published
I close your tomb to a sound
I love — hollow, soft: *whump,*
and give it back to a shelf
and again, someday, I hope, a reader.

RHADAMANTHINE

(inflexibly strict or just)


The word, in this form an adjective, you hear
over and over in your mind, mouth,
dreams, days. You don't know
its meaning,

just its sound, so you look it up
and are disappointed.
You should have known: its thunky rhythm,
the harsh *ra, da,* that pinched *man*

in the middle like a snake spiked
to the ground with a spear,
the whole chop chop of the word.
It was the t-h-i-n-e at the end

which fooled your ear.
You wanted to hear it *thine,*
like the closing of a letter to the beloved,
but it's not, no; it's pronounced *thin.*

## EACH STARTLED TOUCH
## RETURNS THE TOUCH UNSTARTLED

A whole man, half-famished, nailed
to an island. An onshore
wind enters one window

of a narrow cabin
and exits another. *An other,* another
who has been elsewhere, disembarks on this shore

and most of the black night pours
out of them, pours out of them a light
as if from fire coals

or a miner's cap
in a collapsed mine pit,
still lit.

SAY YES

   — *Rachel*


The soul of each silkworm who gave each thread
of silk sings
your blouse

in the other world knowing
it touched you, your — say yes — arms, breasts;
and the wind, between your shoulders,

unsuccessful at being cold,
and the blue water
you lift to your face, each micro-

organism in it
stunned: if consciousness
were assigned,

then these things
would be delirious
desiring — say yes — to touch

any part of you, and glad, a fire-fed-
with-solid-oxygen glad — say yes — to be, in turn,
touched by you.

## CHILDREN IN SCHOOL
## DURING HEAVY SNOWFALL

Not a single footprint in the schoolyard,
the blue-sided drifts
unmolested. Let them out
for recess or lunch and the children
would drive their bodies
through these windblowns, they would charge thigh-, waist-
deep until this snowfield's pocked,

ravaged. . . . Some heads
bob inside, peeping over the sill,
and here and there a taller body, a teacher,
the principal checking the depth,
the wind, the sky. The problem
is: the kids are here and it keeps snowing,
the storm turned this way instead of that.

Now, midday, it's hard to send them home: parents
at work, houses cold, bus driver
overtime pay. A child locked out
or alone inside — firing up
the kerosene heater, the woodstove,
a torch of newspapers,
the drapes lashed with flame.

The principal gets paid to punish
and to decide: might the children burn
or are they buried in snow? He turns
away from the window.
This is New England; winter comes here
every year.

In a major vein shooting blood
to the brain a trombone goes off,
its slide hammering the arterial wall
over and over. Nobody — not the bandleader
with his pointy stick, not
a star-stricken audience — calls
for the trombonist to stand
and take his solo
but once he does
and then sits down again: organic dementia,
maybe aphasia, and you talk to God,
who talks right back,
or you talk to somebody named Dorothy
whom you implore repeatedly
to make a cheese sandwich, please. Not much
will be the same again
after the furniture in the brain
is rearranged: the wrong doily
under the umbrella, the candelabrum
in the stove. What goes on inside
the body is a wonder, Allah,
is a wonder. We who are about to live
tip our sheep to You.

Sixty miles from a lake,
no river or pond within forty-eight,
no ocean near,
and this rowboat, crisply painted, oarlocks
oiled, oars set and cocked,
in a small — mossy, pine needles — clearing
of sparse gray and yellow forest grass.
The light here: like joy, pain, like glass.
On its bow, in red paint, beside the anchor rope,
its name: *A Joy To Be Hidden*
*But a Disaster Not To Be Found.*
An odd place, a long name, for a boat.

The word sounds like the thing.
The sound of the word next to
the sound of another word
sounds like the thing feels
or you desire it to feel. You want
this alive
from its insides
and the mind, the denotative, the dictionary
means naught: what you want
to be known must be known
cellularly, belly-wise,
or on the tongue: *cerulean blue,*
for example, or *punch drunk.*
Those who live elsewhere
than their bodies don't buy it, don't like it,
this in-the-body; the science
and the math tests on it
are yet inconclusive.
There's always this little humming
beneath the surface
of the painting, the dance, the play
(the good ones) that tells your heart
that it — the painting, the dance, the play — tells
a truth: *dewlap, dewlap,*
*it's dawn's time,* it says — the sound
provides the thing its lungs, mouth,
and blood-beat. The sound, the noise of the sound, is
the thing — the deaf can hear it,
the blind see it, this tuning fork
beneath the breastbone, sweetly
accompanying its song.

A handgrenade — *thunk* — lands in a bunker.
Two brave men dive
to smother it with their helmets and bellies,
their heads collide,
both are knocked out
and seconds later die

in the unmuffled blast: hard irony, a device
we turn to
when each door, hatch, gate, path
we turn to
opens to
the blank. And it can make us laugh,

which is good,
human. And it says one thing
when it means another,
which we love: it's safe there, one foot
on each side
of a crevasse, one can be both numb

and acute, brave
and fearful, at ease
in a mink-lined noose: we love
this tool
and the comfort, the justice, it provides,
it provides.

## GLOW WORM

We are all worms but I am a glow worm.

— WINSTON CHURCHILL

Lost in self, drowned; asphyxiated in ego,
blind to same: the dog-
after-a-gut-wagon drivenness, self-righteousness,
all (*the male is small, winged, the female*

*larger, wingless*) to fill
the memory hole
with matter or to extract
from the final bone its marrow.

In spite, the glow worm's inner fire
is chemical, cold, cold,
and therefore false
in drawing others to it for love.

Or leave them
if you have other errands to run — check
your foot
at the shoe store's door (those dogs
too dear to take for granted), their million
baby bones, our pins, our rockets,
those which bear our weight upon the world.
You can buy an arm at the Limb Store,
a bigger one because there's more
you want to hold, and you can leave
some dollars down
for your new hand — there's no better way
to say goodbye, goodbye.
And two doors down, past the airy
lung place, that birdless aviary,
and just beyond the Knees Boutique — step in,
oh do step in
to get your heart checked
by the lady with the angels,
step in, take a number, take a seat,
and she will call your name,
from a million miles away
you will hear your name.

# SNOW AS THE RAIN'S FATHER

*— for Claudia*

What is it up there, back porch to the beyond, what,
up there where the zero resides,
unpierced by radar,
atomic telescope, what
is it? Is this where snow starts, the designs thereof,

before it drops down,
or hailstones,
their layer upon layer
around the perfect, purest ball bearings
at their cores

before they drop down
seeking, specifically, your heart,
that single bone
sizzling in a skillet?
What calls from there?

Or is it a bounceback merely,
a lonely ventriloquial discourse, lament?
And the snow now falling — was it once rain,
a river, sea, or lake,
and before that was it snow again?

# NOTES

The *S.S. Priscilla* and a few phrases of "Boats" belong to Bill Knott. "Emily's Mom" owes a great deal to Cynthia Griffin Wolff's biography *Emily Dickinson*.

" 'Mr John Keats Five Feet Tall' Sails Away": The quoted words in the title are Keats's own.

The italicized line in "A Boat in the Forest" is by Emily Dickinson.